Carole Gerber

Winter Trees

Illustrated by Leslie Evans

ini Charlesbridge

In memory of John D. Engle, Jr.—tree lover, poet, teacher, friend

—C. G.

To Cathy Hawkes and the wonderful winter walks with the dogs

—L. E.

Crunch! We walk through fresh new snow
that sparkles on the frozen ground.
It's peaceful here among the trees—
our footsteps make the only sound.

Trees that once had leaves are bare.
They're dressed instead in lacy white.
Snow dusts their trunks
  and coats their limbs
with flakes that outline them with light.

They stand distinct as skeletons.
We clearly see the form of each:

the egg shape of the maple tree;

the taller oval of the beech . . .

The V formation of the birch;
the yellow poplar, wide and high;

the spreading structure of the oak,
its branches reaching toward the sky.

The sugar maple's bark is gray.
Its twigs are brown. Its buds are stout,
with clawlike tips that in the spring
will burst to shoot new green leaves out.

The beech tree called American
has bark that's smooth and silver-gray.
Tan leaves still cling to limbs and branches
on this cold, bright winter day.

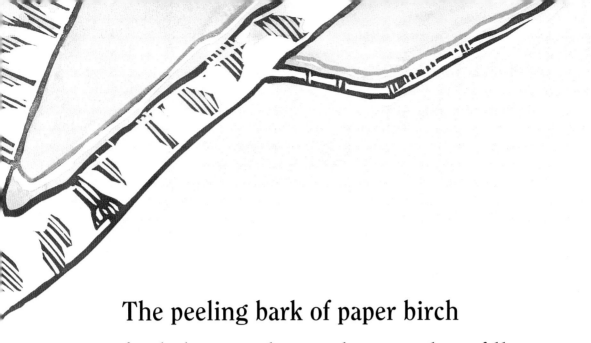

The peeling bark of paper birch
feeds hungry hares that eat their fill.
Inside the trunk, a narrow nest
protects a bird from winter's chill.

Tall yellow poplar's furrowed bark
surrounds a trunk
  that's straight and neat.
Its reddish twigs hold puffy buds—
for deer, a tasty winter treat.

See bur oak's ridged, enormous trunk,
its massive limbs that intertwine,
its tangled twigs that twist and point—
a strange, bewitching tree to find!

The evergreens don't change their look.
We see their needles all year round.
But older needles near the trunk
drop off and fall onto the ground.

Eastern hemlock's sloping branches
droop with tiny twigs and cones.
The hemlock lives for centuries.
Look how huge this tree has grown!

White spruce looks like a pyramid.

Cones hang from branches near the crown.

Don't touch its needles—ouch! They're sharp.

Its scaly bark is grayish brown.

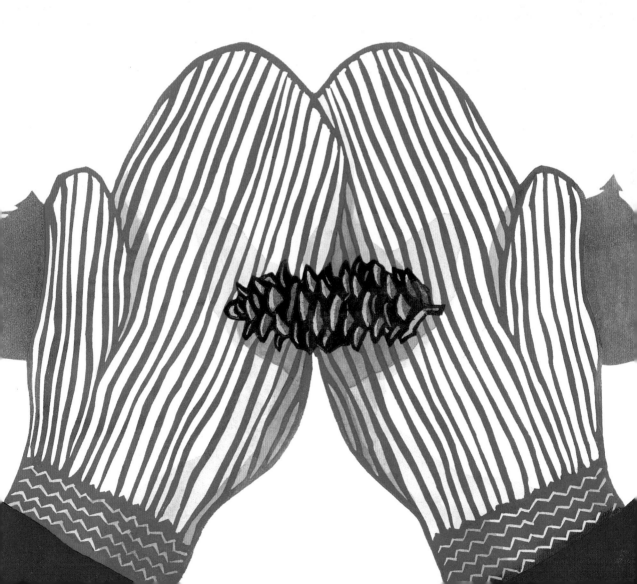

Before we go, let's roll some snow!
We'll make a snowman who will wear
small twigs and pinecones for his face
and leaves from beech trees for his hair.

You can identify trees in winter by looking at the shapes formed by their trunks and bare limbs. Each type of tree has a distinct shape. A tree's bark, twigs, and inactive buds also help identify it in winter. Twigs are the tiny branches that bear buds. These buds can produce leaves, flowers, or both.

The trunks and branches of evergreen trees form distinct shapes, too. Evergreens are covered with thin, pointed leaves called needles. They hold on to their needles all year—making these trees "ever green." Each kind of evergreen has its own color, length, and texture of needles. In spring, the buds on evergreen trees produce tiny branches. Small cones grow on the new branches of some evergreens. Other types of evergreens bear small seeds or berries.

Every tree goes through a similar cycle each year. In spring, new leaves or branches grow from buds. In summer, the tree keeps growing. In autumn, leaves from many types of trees die and fall off. In winter, these trees become dormant, or inactive.

sugar maple

American beech

paper birch

yellow poplar

bur oak

Eastern hemlock

white spruce

Text copyright © 2008 by Carole Gerber
Illustrations copyright © 2008 by Leslie Evans
All rights reserved, including the right of reproduction in whole or in part in any form.
Charlesbridge and colophon are registered trademarks of Charlesbridge Publishing, Inc.

Published by Charlesbridge
85 Main Street
Watertown, MA 02472
(617) 926-0329
www.charlesbridge.com

Library of Congress Cataloging-in-Publication Data
Gerber, Carole.
    Winter trees / Carole Gerber ; illustrated by Leslie Evans.
        p. cm.
    ISBN 978-1-58089-168-4 (reinforced for library use)
1. Trees—Juvenile literature. 2. Trees in winter—Juvenile literature.
I. Evans, Leslie, 1953– ill. II. Title.
QK475.8.G47 2008
582.16—dc22   2007026197

Printed in China
(hc) 10 9 8 7 6 5 4 3 2 1

Illustrations created from linoleum block print, watercolor, and collage, and then digitally enhanced
Display type and text type set in Clearface
Color separations by Chroma Graphics, Singapore
Printed and bound by Toppan Printing Company
Production supervision by Brian G. Walker
Designed by Martha MacLeod Sikkema

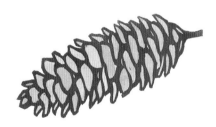